THE COUNT OF MONTE CRISTO

Original story by Alexandre Dumas
Retold by Eleanor Updale
Series Advisor Professor Kimberley Reynolds
Illustrated by Levi Pinfold

OXFORD
UNIVERSITY PRESS

Letter from the Author

I was born in London, and stayed
there for nearly sixty years before
moving to the beautiful city of
Edinburgh, in Scotland. I haven't
always been a writer, but all my
jobs have involved working with
words. For many years, I made
television and radio programmes.

Most of them were about fast-moving news and
political skulduggery, which was good training for
retelling the story of *The Count of Monte Cristo*.

The original book was written in French nearly
200 years ago, but the story is so exciting that
it was soon translated into other languages, so that
people all over the world could hear about
Edmond Dantes and his battle for revenge. The copy
on my bookshelf has more than 1200 pages, in tiny
type. Of course, this short version can only give you a
glimpse of the original. I had to leave out more than I
could keep in. I hope this little book will inspire you
to read the full story one day.

Eleanor Updale

Background

This book is set in France in the first half of the nineteenth century. It was a time of great political turmoil. France had been through a bloody revolution, and its government changed several times. It was always dangerous to be on the losing side. The story begins in 1815, when the former Emperor, Napoleon, was in exile on the island of Elba, near Italy, and his supporters were regarded as outlaws.

It doesn't matter if you don't know the history of the time. The important thing to remember is that sometimes people had to hide their opinions to keep safe. Others didn't have firm views, but supported whoever was in power in order to get money, jobs, or simply to have a quiet life. Greed and corruption were everywhere, whoever was in charge. But kindness and loyalty could find their place, too.

Who is Who?

This story was originally written in French so some of the names may look a bit strange. Mercedes, for example, is a woman, not a car. Many characters adopt new names as their fortunes change. If you get confused, you can look at the following list of characters, but why not skip it for now and dive straight into the adventure?

3

Edmond Dantes
Also known as: Lord Wilmore, Busoni, Sinbad the Sailor and ... The Count of Monte Cristo.

Danglars
Also known as: Baron Danglars.
A sailor in Marseille. Later a banker in Paris.

Monsieur Morrel
A shipowner, Edmond's employer.

Louis Dantes
Edmond's father.

Gaspard Caderousse
A tailor, later an innkeeper.

Mercedes
Edmond's fiancée.

Fernand
Mercedes's cousin. A fisherman,
then a soldier, then a politician.

Monsieur de Villefort
A magistrate in Marseilles.
Later the top prosecutor in Paris.

Faria
A learned man.
A prisoner in the Château d'If.

Jacopo
A sailor who saves Edmond's life and
becomes his most trusted servant.

Franz
A wealthy friend of Albert de Morcerf,
reluctantly engaged to Valentine de Villefort.

Albert de Morcerf
The son of Mercedes and Fernand.

Maximilian Morrel
A soldier, son of the good shipowner.

Valentine de Villefort
Daughter of de Villefort and his first wife.

Madame de Villefort
De Villefort's second wife.

Madame Danglars
Also known as: Baroness Danglars.
Married to Baron Danglars.

Noirtier
De Villefort's father, a notorious
supporter of Napoleon.

Barrois
The faithful servant of Noirtier.

Chapter 1
The Young Captain

As Edmond Dantes steered his ship into Marseille harbour on the last day of February 1815, he was happy. He was only nineteen years old, but he had taken command when the captain died of a fever on the long voyage. Now, thanks to him, the crew were safely home with their valuable cargo. But below decks, one sailor was angry. Danglars, who was more than six years older than Dantes, feared that the ship's owner would make the popular and capable young Dantes the permanent captain. Danglars wanted the job, and the money that went with it, for himself. But before they had even stepped ashore, Danglars was disappointed. The shipowner, Monsieur Morrel, came aboard to break the news.

'Come and dine with me, Edmond. We will celebrate your promotion,' said Morrel, slapping Dantes on the back.

'No thank you, sir,' said Dantes. 'Forgive me, but I must see my father, and then I have some business to attend to.'

Morrel smiled. 'A wedding to arrange, I suppose?'

Edmond blushed. 'Indeed,' he said. 'Mercedes promised she would marry me when I got back, and we need to do it quickly. I must set off for Paris as soon as possible. I have a letter to deliver. It was the captain's dying wish that I should do so.'

Danglars was pretending to sort out the gangplank as he listened in to their conversation. *That letter could be your undoing, Dantes!* he thought. For Dantes had collected it on the island of Elba, where Napoleon Bonaparte, once Emperor of France, was in exile. Danglars knew there would be serious trouble if the letter was discovered. He guessed that it contained a message to Napoleon's supporters, who were plotting to remove the French King from the throne.

'You fool,' he muttered under his breath, knowing that Edmond had no interest in politics and was too honourable to have opened the letter to read it. 'If I had the task of taking that message to Paris, I certainly wouldn't tell a soul.'

Chapter 2
Reunions

Edmond rushed to his father's home in a poor part of town. As they hugged, Edmond could feel old Dantes's ribs through his shirt.

'You haven't been eating,' he said. 'Are you ill?'

'No, no,' said the old man. 'I ran short of money, that's all.'

'But I left you plenty.'

Old Dantes told Edmond how their neighbour, Caderousse the tailor, had taken almost all of it.

'He told me you owed it to him. He threatened to tell Monsieur Morrel about it. I thought you might lose your job.'

'But he agreed that I would repay him when I got back,' shouted Edmond, taking a handful of coins from his pocket. 'See, I have even more money than I was expecting, now that I have been promoted. He's so greedy. You wait till I see him!'

'Please, Edmond, don't smother our happiness with rage. Caderousse may have been hard on me, but I have survived. Let's concentrate on celebrating your return.'

'And my wedding!' said Dantes. 'We'll have the betrothal feast tonight and the ceremony tomorrow.'

His father smiled. 'And does the lovely Mercedes

know of this big rush?'

'She will soon,' said Edmond, grabbing his hat. 'If you don't mind, I'll go to see her straight away.'

Edmond ran down the stairs, full of joy. On the landing he met Caderousse, who greeted him warmly. Edmond forced back the harsh words he wanted to say, and calmly paid off the rest of the debt. His father was right. This happy day should not be ruined by an argument.

Chapter 3
The Anonymous Note

Mercedes had heard that the ship was in, and couldn't disguise her excitement. She rushed to answer the door. But it wasn't Edmond. It was her cousin, Fernand, who had been like a brother to her since they were children. His gloomy look punctured her joy.

'What is it?' she gasped. 'Is it Edmond? Have you brought bad news from the port? Did something happen to him on the voyage?'

'No, he is safe,' said Fernand, adding under his breath, 'more's the pity.'

'Oh, Fernand,' said Mercedes, taking his hand. 'You know I promised to marry Edmond before he went away.'

'You love him more than you love me!'

'I love him in a different way. I'll always be fond of you, Fernand, but I could never be your wife. Please, if you love me, be happy for me.'

Before Fernand could answer, Edmond arrived. Overwhelmed at seeing Mercedes again, he didn't notice Fernand stomping off to a cafe down the street.

Danglars and Caderousse were already at a table outside and Fernand joined them, telling of his sadness at losing Mercedes. Danglars had his own criticisms of Edmond, and even Caderousse moaned about having to lend him money, without admitting that he had taken most of it back from old Dantes almost immediately, and then been paid the rest by Edmond that very day.

The three men talked each other into a throbbing bitterness and when Edmond and Mercedes passed by, arm-in-arm and radiant, their resentment of Dantes's happiness grew worse.

Fernand leaped up. 'I'll kill him,' he hissed.

Danglars pulled him back into his chair and leaned in across the table. 'Calm down,' he said, dropping his voice almost to a whisper. 'You don't need to kill him to stop the marriage. Maybe we could get him arrested.'

'How?' asked Caderousse, leaning in to hear Danglars tell the story of the letter Dantes was carrying.

'It must be something political. If the police knew about it, they would be bound to pick him up,' said Danglars. 'With a bit of luck they'd keep him in long enough to postpone the wedding.' He smiled at Fernand. 'Mercedes might even change her mind. Who knows, Edmond could be in jail till the ship sails again.'

Caderousse smirked. 'With you as captain, no doubt?'

Danglars shrugged in agreement. He called for a pen and paper. Using his left hand to disguise his writing, he composed an anonymous note saying that Dantes was in possession of a treacherous document threatening the King.

Fernand egged him on, but Caderousse was getting worried. 'Come on now, you two,' he said. 'Do you have to do this to him? He's a nice lad. I know his father. This would break the old man's heart.'

Danglars took no notice, and continued writing.

'We all know he's not really a traitor,' said Caderousse. 'He had no choice but to go and collect that letter if it was the captain's dying wish. Surely delivering it to Paris is a good deed, not a bad one? And when did you start caring so much about the King, anyway?'

'I don't give a fig for the King,' said Danglars, pausing to read his handiwork. It looked a bit messy, almost as if it had been written by a child. He doubted whether anyone would take it seriously. Danglars sighed. 'Maybe you're right, Caderousse,' he said, as he screwed the paper into a ball and threw it into a corner. 'Come on, you two. Didn't Dantes say something about a party? If we can't get rid of him, at least we can eat his food!'

'You go ahead,' said Fernand. 'That's no place for me.' He sat slumped at the table until the others were out of sight. Then he jumped up and grabbed the letter from the floor. He smoothed it out. Danglars had already addressed it to the magistrate. Fernand would make sure that it reached its destination.

Chapter 4
The Wedding Feast

Danglars and Caderousse joined in the party as if they wished Mercedes and Edmond the very best for their lives together. Even Fernand turned up eventually, although he sulked menacingly in a corner. Monsieur Morrel was there, proud of his new young captain, and taking good care of Edmond's father, who was sitting in a corner enjoying the fun.

'I have never known such joy,' said Edmond, gazing into Mercedes's glowing eyes. Little did they know that neither of them would ever be that happy again. For Danglars's note had done its work, and the police were at the door.

'Where is Edmond Dantes?' shouted the officer.

Caderousse caught Fernand's eye. A quick nod from Fernand was enough for Caderousse to guess why the police had come.

Edmond stepped forward. 'I am Dantes,' he said. 'How can I help you?'

'You are under arrest,' said the officer, as Edmond's friends and family gasped.

'But why?' asked Edmond, not even bothering to struggle as a policeman bound his hands. 'There must be a mistake. Is there some problem with the customs documents for the ship?'

Caderousse sidled up to Danglars at the back of the room. 'Fernand must have sent that note,' he whispered. 'We have to explain that it was only a joke. We can't let them take Edmond away.'

Danglars grabbed Caderousse's collar and pulled him closer. 'Keep quiet. They know about the letter to Paris now. If we say we wrote the note, they'll think we are in on the plot too. We will be in prison before we know it.'

'But we have to stop this!' said Caderousse.

Danglars squeezed his arm, painfully. 'Not a word, d'you hear?'

Caderousse held his tongue as Edmond was led away. The young bridegroom had a forced smile as he tried to reassure his father and Mercedes.

'Don't worry,' he shouted over his shoulder, 'I haven't done anything wrong. I'm sure this can be cleared up in no time. Enjoy yourselves. I'll be back soon.'

Monsieur Morrel poured a glass of water for old Dantes, who was dizzy with shock. He beckoned to Mercedes. 'Take care of him,' said Morrel. 'I'm going to the town hall to see what this is all about. Trust me; I won't rest until you have your Edmond back.'

Chapter 5
The Interview

The chief magistrate was away, so the interview was conducted by his deputy, Monsieur de Villefort, an ambitious man, not much older than Edmond himself. As it happened, de Villefort had been called away from his own wedding feast. It was a grander affair than Edmond's, but shorter on fun. De Villefort was marrying into a well-born family whose fortune and connections would help his career. He needed all the social support he could get, for he was trying to shake off his father's reputation as a political firebrand, gained when the monarchy had been overthrown and bloody revolution swept France. De Villefort had even changed his name in the hope of making people forget the link. As a magistrate, he was building a reputation for being severe with opponents of the King. His bride was a sweet girl, who, as he left their reception, begged him to be merciful to the suspect he was about to interview.

On the way into the town hall, de Villefort was stopped by Monsieur Morrel, who told him all Edmond's good points and insisted, when told of the charges against him, that Dantes could never be a traitor. De Villefort was inclined to believe him, not least because he was keen to get back to his party. So, as the interview progressed, he was glad to see that the case against the prisoner was pretty flimsy.

De Villefort read the anonymous note. It struck him as a rather amateur creation: very obviously in a disguised hand. Morrel had told him about Dantes's wedding. Perhaps this was a trick by the bridegroom's friends, a jape that had got out of control. He questioned Dantes about the scribbled allegations.

'Is it true that you deliberately diverted your ship to the isle of Elba, knowing that the former Emperor was there?'

'Yes, sir. I did,' said Dantes. 'I delivered a package from my captain. It was his last instruction to me before he died of a fever.'

'And the contents of that package?'

'I have no idea. It was not my place to look. I was simply the messenger.'

De Villefort was impressed with the prisoner's calm and open manner. Dantes struck him as someone so trusting that he could easily get into trouble by accident. But was he really a traitor? There was no evidence of that.

De Villefort looked back at the note. 'It says here that you returned with a letter.'

'Indeed,' said Dantes. 'I am leaving straight after my wedding to deliver it to Paris.'

By now, de Villefort was confident that the letter would lead him to any conspirators. There would be no need to detain the nervous bridegroom. De Villefort could get back to his own bride and reassure her that her plea for mercy had been granted.

'Do you have the letter with you now?' he said.

'It's here,' said Dantes, gesturing with his bound hands towards the inside pocket of his jacket. 'I am to take it to Monsieur Noirtier, Rue Coq-Héron ... '

Unseen by Dantes, de Villefort's lips moved in silent synchronization with Edmond's as he said the door number, 'Thirteen.'

Having slipped the letter from Edmond's pocket, de Villefort took a step back, out of the prisoner's eyeline. He checked the address. It was as Dantes had said. He paced up and down, reading the contents and muttering unintelligibly to himself. Dantes was dreading what de Villefort would say next, but when he spoke, his words were serious, but his tone was friendly.

'Well, Dantes,' said de Villefort. 'This does not look good for you, does it?'

'I'm not sure, sir. I swear, I am a humble seaman, and all I wish is to rejoin my bride at our wedding feast.'

'I understand,' said de Villefort. 'Tell me now, can I take your word that you were given nothing else on Elba? No verbal messages?'

'No, sir.'

'So this letter, of which you do not know the contents,

is the only evidence against you?'

'That's right.'

'So if I were to destroy this letter, we would be sure it would never reach its destination, and there would be no case for you to answer?'

Without waiting for a reply, de Villefort leaned forward and pushed a corner of the paper into the fire. He raised it up, and saw the flame licking against the address. The words *Monsieur Noirtier, Rue Coq-Héron* were no more.

'See,' he said. 'That is your wedding present from me! I have disposed of the evidence. All we have now is an anonymous note. I cannot tell who it was from, so I cannot question them. There is no reason why you shouldn't go free.'

Dantes fell to his knees. 'Thank you, sir. You are too kind.'

'There are just a few administrative details to sort out. I must keep you in custody for a little longer, but trust me. You will see your bride again soon.'

He rang a bell on his desk, and a guard came to the door. Dantes could not hear their whispered conversation, but he was almost crying with relief and gratitude. As armed guards led him out to a courtyard and bundled him into a carriage, he shouted his thanks

to de Villefort, who was pulling on his gloves as he strode
back to his party.

Chapter 6
An Unexpected Journey

Dantes didn't take much notice of where the carriage was going until he realized that they must be very close to the shore. He had been expecting a short trip to the cells, but before he knew it, he was in a small boat. The guards took to the oars and rowed across the dark water. Edmond was puzzled. Where were they taking him? Why were they at sea when he had to be at his wedding in just a few hours? None of his questions received an answer until the one which, in his horror, he could have answered himself. He had his back to the horizon, and had watched in desperation as the lights of the harbour receded and then disappeared. Somehow he could feel a huge, cold presence looming up behind him. He tried to turn to look, but his shackles held him firm.

'Where are we?' he asked, although the seas around Marseille were so familiar to him that he knew, even though he didn't want to believe it. He was well aware that, almost within touching distance, a vertical wall of rock pierced the black waves, and that at its top was a fortress whose reputation chilled the hearts of all who knew it.

At last, one of the guards spoke. 'It's the Château d'If,' he said. 'Our destination. Take your last breaths of freedom, son. Not many come out of there!'

'No! There's been a mistake,' Edmond shouted against
the wind. But the guards were tying up the boat at a jetty
where fearsome sentries stood with flaming torches.
No more words were spoken until Edmond, wrestling
against the strong arms of his captors, heard a vast door
slam behind him, and the sound of bolts sliding and keys
turning. How could this be? He was inside the most
notorious prison in the south of France. He had to find
a way to get a message to Monsieur de Villefort. Clearly
one of the guards had misunderstood the magistrate's
instructions.

Chapter 7
The Château d'If

The turnkey was unimpressed by Edmond's pleas of innocence. 'Do you think I haven't heard that before?' he said lazily, as he dragged Dantes towards his cell. 'It's what they all say.'

'I want to see the governor!' screamed Dantes.

The reply was a surly shrug.

Furious, bemused and scared, Dantes lurched forwards, accidentally knocking the man's head against the stone wall. The turnkey wiped his sleeve against his nose to soak up the blood.

'You'll see the governor now, all right,' he mumbled, taking away the small rushlight as he closed the door behind him.

Edmond was alone in the cell, in total darkness. He felt his way round the damp walls, but could find nowhere to sit except the filthy floor. He slumped down, feeling small creatures brushing against his body as he allowed his tears to fall.

The burst of light when the door was opened for the governor hurt Edmond's eyes so much that he couldn't make out the man's features. In a torrent of words, he apologized for striking the guard, and begged to be allowed to send a message to Monsieur de Villefort.

The governor wasn't interested.

'Your sentence will be increased,' he said.

'Sentence?' said Dantes, mystified. 'I have no sentence. I have not been tried. I have not committed a crime.' In his anxiety, he raised his bound hands again. Fearing Dantes would lash out at the governor, two guards grabbed him and dragged him towards the door.

'Dungeon?' said one.

'He's dangerous,' said the other.

'Dungeon!' said the governor. 'And half rations till he mends his manners.'

Dantes was manhandled down spiral stairs and narrow corridors. With each step, the air grew more sour and the darkness almost tangible as the damp took possession of his clothes and hair. Soon he was alone. He cried out, but no answer came. His shin bumped against something hard. It had the shape of a narrow bed. His fingers caught the edge of a sodden strip of fabric. He guessed that it must once have been a blanket, and that the putrid bag of straw beneath it was meant to serve as a mattress. He couldn't bear the idea of lying on it. In any case, he felt it would be a betrayal of Mercedes, his father, and all his friends to give in to the exhaustion that now consumed him. He shouldn't sleep. He should find a way out. But the Château d'If had played a part in horror stories since his boyhood. Edmond Dantes knew he was trapped, but he didn't know why.

Chapter 8
A Companion

Six years passed. Guards came and went, some kinder (or at least, less cruel) than others. One talked a little when he was sure no one else could hear, and told of another prisoner who had been in the dungeons four years longer than Dantes. No one could remember why that man had been imprisoned, though it was said to be something political he had done in Italy. But it didn't matter. The man had quite lost his mind, according to the turnkey. He believed himself to be in possession of a great fortune and would regularly offer millions of francs in return for his freedom.

Dantes started to listen out for sounds from the other cell, but the walls were thick and there were no human noises, though rats scrabbled invisibly, especially at night, and sometimes a gull taking a rest on its way across the bay would squawk somewhere out of sight. There was no window in the cell, only a small opening for air and a little light, high up at the end of a channel carved through the stone. It was as wide as a man's head at the inside wall, but only the size of a fist where it opened to the sea. There was no way out.

Then one night, after the last visit from the guard, Dantes heard an unfamiliar sound coming from the wall near his bed. It was a continual scratching noise, as if made by a huge claw, a powerful tooth, or some iron tool attacking the stones. Dantes tapped out a rhythm on the wall. There was a pause, and then the same rhythm clicked back. He tried again. There was no doubt about it. A human being was close by. Dantes dragged his bed away from the wall, smashed his water jug and used a shard to pick at the mortar between the stones.

It was painfully slow, but in the Château d'If the only thing the inmates possessed was time. Because Edmond had smashed his jug, the jailer took to bringing water in a metal saucepan and Edmond used the handle as a lever to try to move the stones. After hours of digging, he would replace the loose rocks and push his bed back into position to hide his work. One night, he hit an obstruction and cried out in despair. Another voice answered.

Dantes shouted back. 'Who's there?' he called. 'Speak again, though the sound of your voice terrifies me.'

The voice did speak. 'Who are you?'

'An unhappy prisoner. A Frenchman,' Dantes replied.

'I am Faria, from Italy. Tell me, where are you tunnelling from?' said the voice.

'From the floor behind my bed,' said Dantes.

There was a pause, and a sigh. 'Then my calculations were not correct. I took this for the outside wall of the prison. I was going to break through and throw myself into the sea. Instead, I have only reached another cell.'

The man's dejection was matched only by Edmond's elation at hearing a human voice. His mind filled with thoughts of companionship – and maybe tunnelling to escape together.

'Don't give up,' he said. 'We have each other now. Keep going so we can meet, talk, and be friends.'

The two men dug with new vigour until one day, almost without warning, the last of the stones and earth that divided them fell away, and up through the floor of Edmond's cell came the head, then the shoulders, and then the thin, lithe body of a man. His hair and beard were long, grey and dirty; his clothes were little more than rags.

Edmond was startled by his wild appearance, until he realized that had there been a mirror in his cell, this was the image he would see. His hair might be a little darker, that was all.

Faria was excited to be somewhere new. 'If I stood on your shoulders, I could see out,' he said. 'Perhaps we could dig through to the sea from here.'

Groaning at the unusual exertion, Dantes hoisted Faria up.

'Oh no,' said Faria. 'It is as I feared. This wall leads to an inner courtyard.' He dropped down from Dantes's shoulders. 'You should take exercise, young man. If we are going to escape together you should keep yourself strong.'

'Do you take exercise? Apart from the tunnelling, I mean.'

'Oh yes. And I attend to more than my body. I look after my mind too. Come through to my cell, and I will show you what I do.'

Chapter 9
In Faria's Cell

The two of them slithered through the tunnel. Edmond was startled when he emerged. The walls of Faria's chamber were covered in hieroglyphics: strange markings Dantes could not understand.

'I will explain everything in time,' said Faria. 'Some of those marks are my clock. See how that beam of light from my tiny window strikes the wall? It moves along as the day goes by. It means I know when the guards might come, and when it is safe to dig. At other times, I write. I write of history and of the future, to take me away from the present. I am working on *A Treatise on the Practicability of Forming Italy into One General Monarchy*. And I am doing calculations that will challenge the very foundations of mathematics.'

'You say you are writing. You have a pen, ink, paper?'

'Of my own devising. And hidden.' Faria removed a loose brick from the wall and took out some objects. 'You may know, perhaps, that the guards think I have lost my mind?' He waved away Edmond's assurance that he disagreed. 'No, no, that belief serves me well. They give me little extras out of sympathy, to indulge me. I get a little wine on Sundays. I mix it with soot from that old chimney.' He pointed to a grate in the far wall, which had clearly gone unused for decades. 'It makes the most satisfactory ink.'

'And paper?'

'I have found a way to make linen as smooth as parchment.'

'But where do you get the linen?'

'I tear strips from my sheets.'

'Don't the guards notice?'

'I cut them little by little, and hem the rough edges, using thread from my shirts and needles I make myself.'

'Needles?' Edmond was astounded. 'You make needles? How?'

'You know that bony fish they give us sometimes?'

'More bones than fish, I'd say.'

'Well, that's just as well for me,' said Faria. 'I use the small bones to make needles and the bigger ones for my pens.' He handed Dantes the long backbone of a fish that had been trimmed and sharpened so that the nib was as fine as any bought in a shop.

'You must have had a knife to do this,' said Edmond. 'Where did you get it?'

Faria went to the other side of the cell and levered out another stone. 'It wouldn't do to have everything hidden in the same place,' he said. 'I split things up in case someone ever comes looking.' He put his hand into the hole in the wall and pulled out two gleaming knives.

'I fashioned them from the metal fastenings under my bed,' he said. 'It took me years to sharpen them.'

Dantes weighed the bigger knife in his hand. 'But if you've got this, you could kill the guard,' he said.

'I could not!' said Faria. 'I couldn't kill anyone. Even my freedom would not be worth that. To live in freedom with a life on my conscience would be worse than to stay here.'

Dantes stared at the blade. 'I seem to remember that I once had as pure a heart as yours,' he said. 'I am not so sure of it now.'

'You would kill those who betrayed you? Do you think of them in the long cold nights?'

'I don't know who they were. I don't know why I'm here.'

'Surely you must have some notion? Was nothing said when you were arrested?'

'I was accused of being a supporter of Napoleon,' said Dantes. 'I was questioned about a letter I was carrying to Paris. But the magistrate, Monsieur de Villefort, accepted my innocence. He even burned the letter that was the only evidence against me. He promised that I would be released.'

Chapter 10
The Penny Drops

Faria asked Dantes more about the circumstances surrounding his arrest. Edmond talked of his father, his wedding, his friends and his good employer, Monsieur Morrel.

'And you really have no idea who wrote that anonymous note?'

Dantes shook his head.

Faria patted his hand. 'I'm sure we can work it out,' he said. 'Think. Who stood to gain if you disappeared?'

Dante shrugged. 'No one.'

'Really? What of that Danglars of whom you spoke? He served under you on your ship?'

'Yes. I didn't like him much, but he was a good worker.'

'And if you had not been made captain?' asked Faria.

'Oh, it would certainly have been him.'

'And he knew you had the letter?'

'Of course, he would have seen me carry it aboard at Elba.'

Faria raised an eyebrow as, for the first time, the truth began to dawn in Edmond's mind. Faria continued.

'And the cousin of Mercedes?'

'Fernand. Yes. He was certainly angry about our wedding. Come to think of it, I saw him with Danglars and Caderousse that day. They looked as if they were plotting something. But this? No, surely not. And anyway, that anonymous letter didn't work. De Villefort didn't believe it. He wanted to let me go. He burned the letter, remember?'

'Yes. That's interesting. What do you remember of that letter?'

'Nothing. I didn't read it. All I saw was the address.'

'Which was?'

'Monsieur Noirtier, Rue Coq-Héron 13.'

'Ah!' exclaimed Faria. 'Now we have it. Noirtier.'

'Who is he?'

'My dear Dantes, you are so young! Noirtier was once among the most famous republicans in France, an implacable enemy of the King. You were at great risk carrying a document bearing his name. But more to the point, Noirtier was so notorious that his own son disowned him. He left Paris, moved to Marseille, became a respectable magistrate, and changed his name to—'

'De Villefort!' said Dantes, who at last realized that the man in whom he had placed so much hope was, in fact, the source of his trouble.

'No wonder he burned the letter. I fear, dear Edmond, that it was not to save you, but to save his own reputation if anyone recalled his old surname. With you locked up in here and the evidence destroyed, no one would ever know that de Villefort's father was corresponding with the Emperor Napoleon.'

Dantes was still pulling everything together. 'And without Danglars and Fernand, and maybe Caderousse too, de Villefort would never have known I had the letter.'

'Exactly.'

Dantes paced around Faria's cell, too enraged to speak.

'I should not have talked about this,' said Faria. 'I have made you unhappy.'

'Unhappy? How could I be more miserable than I am already, locked up here, with no hope of release?'

'Or of escape, it would seem. My attempt failed. There is no way out.'

'No, we must press on, Faria,' Dantes said with determination. 'Together, we will find a way. We will keep digging. And while we are working, you will teach me everything you know. I can see you are a wise man. You can make me fit for the task of revenge that lies ahead when I get out of here.'

'I will teach you, Edmond. But I will impart my knowledge for its own sake, and not for use in the black art of revenge. If you go down that path, you will regret it, I promise you.' Faria put the knives and pens back in their hiding places, and lightened the tone of his voice. 'But we must talk more about all this tomorrow. The guard will be here soon. Go back to your cell now, and visit me again after breakfast. Be sure to cover your entrance to the tunnel so nobody can see.'

'I will,' said Dantes, calming down. 'Thank you Faria. Thank you for being my friend.'

Dantes went back through the tunnel and replaced his bed so that nothing unusual was visible. He lay down on his back and watched drips of water forming on the ceiling. As each dropped to the floor he spat out a name. 'Danglars! Fernand! Caderousse! De Villefort! I trusted you. How could I have been so blind?'

Chapter 11
Life Outside

N one of the men Dantes was cursing was still in Marseille. In the years since his arrest, their lives had changed, too.

De Villefort was prospering in Paris. After burning the letter, he had realized that he could use its contents to his advantage. He had rushed to break the news that Napoleon planned to escape from Elba, raise an army, and force the King off the throne.

A little later, de Villefort regretted destroying the letter because Napoleon's plan succeeded and he ruled France once more. So de Villefort was on the losing side, and had to hide away. If the letter had still been in his possession, he could have pretended to be one of Napoleon's supporters, and he would happily have lied to be in favour with the new government. But de Villefort was lucky. Napoleon was overthrown after just one hundred days, and de Villefort re-emerged from obscurity.

When the King returned, de Villefort was rewarded for his apparent loyalty with riches and high office. He had a fine house, and a sweet young daughter. He never let himself think about the innocent man whose imprisonment in the Château d'If made his comfortable life possible.

Fernand had joined the army and was sent abroad to fight. At first, Mercedes refused to marry him. She insisted on waiting for Edmond and caring for his dying father. Fernand was very successful in his military campaigns, always managing to switch sides at the right moment to stay in favour. He would even trick and betray allies if it meant his personal fortune would increase. When old Dantes died, Mercedes, who was now convinced that Edmond must be dead too, finally agreed to marry Fernand.

Danglars got his wish and became captain of the ship but his employer, Monsieur Morrel, never forgot about Edmond Dantes, and was always talking about him, trying to find out where he was and why he had been imprisoned. Those frequent reminders meant Danglars's conscience could not rest, so he told his employer, Morrel, that he wanted to leave the sea and take a job on shore.

Out of kindness, Morrel found him a job as a cashier with a banker in Spain. Danglars was soon obsessed with making money, bending the rules and cheating to amass a huge fortune. He started his own banking business, lending money to the French nobility. Eventually he joined them, becoming Baron Danglars based in a mansion in Paris.

As for Caderousse, he did not have such good fortune, and he often thought of Dantes. He knew that he should have stopped the others writing the note that had condemned him, and that he could have spoken up when Edmond was arrested. He despised himself for being a coward, but he had other things to worry about now.

He was married to a greedy and dissatisfied woman, and at her insistence he had bought an inn on a country road outside Marseille. The business was not a success, and she never let him forget it.

Chapter 12
Faria's Secret

L ying on his bed in his cell, Edmond knew nothing of this. He pictured his old friends just as he had known them, except that they were no longer friends. His mind raced through ideas for punishing their treachery. There was only one consolation. At last he had a companion in the prison, and as soon as the guard finished his rounds the next morning, he wriggled through the tunnel to visit Faria again.

Faria greeted him with an apology. 'I have been worrying about you all night, Dantes, and blaming myself. I should never have sown the seeds of anger in your heart.'

'No, my dear Faria, all you did was make me see the truth. And in a strange way, you have also given me hope. I have something to live for now. I will escape, and I will get my revenge.'

'Then I will help you. I will redo my calculations, and see if we can find a way through the wall. We will work together.'

'And while we are working, I want to know about you. How did you come by all your knowledge?'

'I was employed for many years as a tutor for a wealthy and learned family in Rome. I was in charge of their library and I read and re-read many books. I still do read them.'

Dantes looked around the empty cell, bemused.

Faria chuckled. 'In my head. I know them by heart after so many years of study.'

'Will you teach them to me?' asked Dantes. 'What are their subjects?'

'Everything, from politics and philosophy to mathematics and medicine. You will be an expert on all those things, and more, by the time our new tunnel is dug.'

'Are there stories, too?' Edmond asked.

'Many. Some from exotic lands, but none so strange and wonderful as the true story I will tell you one day of a great fortune that is waiting for us when we escape. We will have wealth beyond imagining.'

Dantes remembered how, long ago, a guard had told him that Faria was mad, believing that he could bribe his way out of the prison with millions in gold. Had the guard been right? Was Faria a genius or a sad, deluded fool?

Over the next eight years, that question was answered. Faria's knowledge was indeed profound, and he gradually passed on much of it. Edmond learned new languages. Faria told him about art and history, and taught him the recipes for strange remedies dating back centuries. One was the formula for a poisonous potion that could kill or revive, depending on how much of it was used.

But Faria was ageing. He had already been in the Château d'If for years when Dantes had arrived. Only the hope of escape had kept him alive for so long, and now his body was calling out for death.

'I will not be here to see you finish the tunnel,' he said to Dantes. 'But I know you will get out of here one day. I want to tell you about the treasure and how to find it.'

Dantes still believed the treasure to be a fantasy, but he didn't want to upset the old man, so he sat beside him on the bed while Faria told his tale.

'The family I worked for in Italy, the Spadas, were very rich,' he said, in a faint and husky voice. 'And they had been even richer in the Middle Ages. But Italy has always been a dangerous country. Worse, even, than France. Riches had to be kept safe. If you were wealthy centuries ago, it was no good having money in a bank. You needed coins, and gold, and jewels that could be picked up and carried away to safety if your life was threatened, or someone seized your land.'

'And the Spadas had to flee?'

'Yes, in the fifteenth century, though they returned to Rome eventually, and my employer built up a new fortune of his own. The old family treasures had been hidden somewhere no one would ever find them without precise directions. The story of that treasure was passed down through generations of the family, but the map was lost. My employer was the very last of the line. He had no one to pass the treasure to. It doesn't belong to anyone now.

We can take it.'

'But what is the use of knowing that if we don't have the map?'

'But that's what I want to tell you. There is no map!'

Dantes heart sank. He had been allowing his mind to run with the idea of finding untold riches. Maybe the guard had been right about Faria. On this subject, Faria's mind was deranged.

Faria sensed Dantes's disappointment. A cheeky smile crept across his old face. 'There is no map, but there is this!' he whispered, opening his hand to reveal a small scrap of paper, tightly rolled into a cylindrical shape.

'Take it. Look at it,' he said.

Edmond unrolled the paper. It was dirty, and burned at the edges. The faint writing appeared to say:

This treasure, which may amount to two
of Roman crowns in the most distant c
of the second opening wh
declare to belong
to him alo
heir.
  25th April, 149

'But this is meaningless!' said Edmond.

'To you, my friend, but not to me. Let me explain how I came upon that paper. I told you that the last of the Spadas had no heirs. We had become close as master and secretary, and he left his great library to me. Shortly after his death, I was sorting out the manuscripts and needed some extra light. I reached for a scrap of paper and caught it in the fire so I could light the lamp. As soon as the flame took hold, I could see words upon the paper. They must have been written in a secret ink that only gained colour when exposed to heat. I managed to read the whole message before the flame had eaten half of it away. I have kept the remains, but in my head I know it all.'

'So you have the full instructions?'

'Indeed I do, and I shall pass them on to you now, for they are of no use to a dying man.'

'Don't talk of death, ' said Dantes. 'You are only sick. You will recover.'

'No, my friend. We both know that I am near my end. Do not let politeness keep you from a fortune. I have taken too long with my story already. The guard will be here soon, and you must get back to your cell.'

'I am listening,' said Dantes.

'The complete message says that the treasure is hidden on the island of Monte Cristo. It is in the far corner of the second cave. I was on my way there when I was arrested. Unless someone else has stumbled across it, it is waiting for you.'

'I know Monte Cristo,' said Edmond. 'I have sailed past it a hundred times. It is uninhabited. There is nothing there but wild goats.'

'Then go, my friend, if you get the chance. I know that opportunity will never be mine. Now be quick. Get back to your cell.'

Edmond dipped a corner of his shirt into the rusty bowl on the floor, and gently dabbed water against the old man's lips. Faria's eyes closed. Edmond bent over and kissed him on the forehead. Then he dived back down the tunnel to his own cell, not knowing whether his beloved friend was alive or dead.

Chapter 13
A Death in the Prison

Edmond didn't have to wait long to find out. Soon there were more footsteps than usual in the corridor outside his cell. He couldn't make out what was being said, so he took a chance and went back into the tunnel to listen in to the conversations around Faria's bed. The governor was there, and a doctor had been called to certify the death. It amused Dantes how death was the only reason for an inmate of Château d'If to be visited by a medical man.

'Prepare the body now,' said the governor. 'But we'll take it out in the morning.'

'Yes sir,' said the familiar voice of the turnkey. 'I'll need some help to carry him, though.'

'I will make arrangements,' said the governor, as he and the doctor left.

For a moment, Dantes was paralyzed with fear. What if they looked into his cell on their way out? But then he heard their steps on the stairs, and their voices dying away as the governor and the doctor climbed up from the dungeons. There were shuffling noises from Faria's cell, then a few thumps and gasps. The turnkey was doing something to the body. Then there came another voice.

'That's it for now. I'll see you in the morning.'

'Do you think I should stay and guard him tonight?' the turnkey replied.

'He never gave you any trouble when he was alive. I don't suppose he will be running off now he's dead. We've got a card game going in the guard room upstairs. Why not come and join us?'

Dantes frantically wriggled back down the tunnel. He had to return to his cell and rearrange the bed before the guards passed his door. He was still only part of the way out of the hole in the floor when he heard their voices outside his door.

'With all that fuss, this one never got any supper. I left the bread and water in the other cell,' said the turnkey.

His friend was keen to get upstairs. 'Don't hang about. One night without any food won't hurt him. You can give him double in the morning, now the old man's gone. Come on, I can't stand this stench of death. It gives me the creeps. Let's get going.'

Never had Dantes been so glad to go without food. He pulled himself up into the cell, and pushed his bed back over the hole. The tunnel had no use now. He would have to block up the opening to make sure it was never found. Then he realized that the guards might find it from the other end, perhaps as early as tomorrow morning. He pulled the bed away again. He would have to go back into Faria's cell and make sure the entrance couldn't be detected. At least, he thought, he would have one more chance to look upon the face of his only friend.

Chapter 14
The Switch

Dantes looked down on Faria's body, but he couldn't see his face. The corpse had been sewn into a rough sack and left on the bed. Edmond imagined the guards tossing it into an unmarked grave with none of the respect that the learned old man deserved. Tears came. They were the first he had shed since the early days of his captivity. They were tears for Faria, but also for himself, alone again, perhaps for the rest of his life.

But then an idea crept into his head. Within minutes, it had formed into a plan. He would take Faria's place inside the sack, and dig his way out of the grave when the guards had gone. It was worth a try. If it didn't work, how could lying underground until he suffocated be worse than spending the rest of his natural life in the dungeon?

He unpicked the thread that closed the sack and, apologizing to the corpse for his roughness, lugged Faria's body through to his own cell, where he arranged it on his bed, face to the wall, as if in a deep sleep. He pulled the bed towards the wall behind him as he worked his way backwards through to Faria's cell. There, he opened the old man's secret compartment and took the large sharp knife, ready to cut his way out of the grave the next day. He threaded one of Faria's fish-bone needles with the cord that had secured the sack and shuffled inside it, sewing it closed from the inside. Then he lay on the bed, and waited.

He didn't expect to sleep, and yet he was woken by the sound of the guards coming into the cell. There were several of them. He recognized their voices from the night before. Clutching the knife to his chest, he kept himself as still as he could as they manhandled the sack up the stairs. The blast of fresh air that greeted him as they went outside almost made him gasp, but he stopped himself, knowing that the slightest movement could cost him his life. His ears could hardly bear the noise of the wind and the waves – the loudest sounds he had heard for fourteen years. He steeled himself for being dropped into the grave, hoping that the men had been too lazy to dig it deep.

'Ready?' said the voice of one of the guards.

'Ready,' said another.

'On three.'

'One!'

The guards began to swing the sack.

'Two!' Another swing, and Dantes braced himself to hit the bottom of the grave, determined not to show any sign of life, no matter how hard he fell.

'Three!'

There was no sudden impact. Instead, Dantes found himself flying through the air. In an instant, he realized what had happened. There was no grave. He had been thrown over the battlements. Would he hit the rock at the bottom, or had they thrown him hard and far enough to reach the sea? He tumbled like a wounded bird towards the waves. He couldn't help himself; a roar of terror sang out from his lungs. By a reflex he took a mighty breath in just as the sack slapped into the icy waves.

Dantes worked fast. With Faria's sharpest knife, he tore through the fabric of the sack. Some strange animal instinct for survival gave him the power to kick his way upwards. But he ached with pain, fighting the urge to inhale again. At last, the waves parted above his head and he gulped down the most delicious air he would ever taste. Edmond Dantes was free.

Chapter 15
Stranded

He was free, but he was not safe. He could not risk swimming towards Marseille, where they might be on the lookout for him. It would only be a matter of time before the guards noticed that 'Dantes' had not moved from his bed, and discovered Faria's corpse there in his place. Once the alarm was raised, and perhaps a reward offered for his capture, he could not ask strangers for help. He swam instead towards the uninhabited isle of Tiboulen, using his training as a navigator to get there, keeping a distant lighthouse to his right all the time. It took him more than an hour to reach the deserted beach. He staggered for a few weary footsteps, and then fell, exhausted, to the sand. He silently thanked Faria for making him exercise in prison. Without that advice, he would never have survived. But all his strength, and more, had been used. He closed his eyes and fell into a deep, but sweet, sleep.

He was woken by a flash of lightning and a roll of thunder. A storm was straight overhead. Dantes pulled himself into the shelter of some rocks. With each flash, he could see the outline of a ship struggling to stay upright on the tempestuous waves. All of his sailor's instincts made him want to help the poor souls on board. No one who made his living on the seas would ever pass by another seaman in trouble. But there was nothing he could do.

At first light, the fate of the ship became clear. The waves were gentle now, but as each lapped the shore, it carried driftwood from the stricken vessel. There were bodies, too. The storm had been unkind. But it had brought Dantes what he needed. Rainwater had collected amongst the granite rocks, and Edmond was able to quench his raging thirst. He watched over the waves for survivors, and soon caught sight of another ship. With his experienced eye, he could tell that it was Italian. He waved.

But why would anyone be looking out towards an uninhabited island? As the ship grew nearer, Dantes saw his chance. He took the hat from one of the dead sailors, thanking him as he did so, and chose the largest piece of debris for a raft. With another for a paddle, he made his way toward the ship, shouting, and waving his hat as he got closer.

He thought they would never spot him, but at last they did, and a lifeboat was lowered from the side to rescue him. A sailor hauled him in by his long hair and then he was pulled by a rope up onto the ship. The amazement in the crew's eyes when they saw the bedraggled figure before them made Dantes realize for the first time what he must look like after fourteen years in the Château d'If.

'My ship was wrecked last night,' he said. 'I think I may be the only survivor.'

'We will stay a while, and look for others,' said the captain. 'But we must get on our way to Livorno before the weather turns again.' He called to the man who had pulled Dantes from the sea. 'Jacopo, get our friend dry clothes and a hammock.'

Jacopo took Dantes below decks and gave him some of his own clothes.

'What is the name of this ship?' Dantes asked.

'*La Jeune Amelie*,' Jacopo replied.

'And your cargo?'

'Oh, we carry what we can, when we can, wheresoever we must.'

Dantes realized they were smugglers, landing goods at out of the way places to avoid paying taxes at the official ports. It cheered him. These men wanted to stay clear of the authorities. They were unlikely to give him away if the alarm sounded from the Château d'If. He had one more question for Jacopo.

'That storm has made me completely lose track of time. What is the date today?'

'28th February, 1829,' said Jacopo.

Dantes just nodded. Fourteen years to the day since his arrest. He had been nineteen then. He was thirty-three now. The thought of those who had stolen the years from him lurched again in his heart.

La Jeune Amelie sailed around for a while, finding plenty of debris, which made Edmond's story believable, but there was not a living soul in the water. Then they turned for Italy as Dantes slept again, lulled by the familiar rocking of a ship and the creaking of timbers for the first time in fourteen years. A cannon blast rang out from the Château d'If. A prisoner had escaped from the most notorious jail in France. *Good luck to him, wherever he is*, thought the captain, without changing course.

Chapter 16
Amongst Friends

The next day, of course, everybody wanted to know more about their unexpected passenger. Dantes told them all about his career at sea, without saying that it had ended abruptly when he was only nineteen. He thought the sailors would treat him better if he made himself useful, so he put his knowledge of the local waters to great use, saving them time by sailing closer to some rocks than they would have dared, and telling them stories about the places they passed.

'Where do you want to get to?' asked the captain.

'I would be happy if you were to drop me at the first inhabited place,' said Dantes, 'but happier still if I could join your crew and sail to Livorno. I lost all my money in the wreck. I need to earn more as soon as I can.'

The captain was impressed by Dantes's seamanship, so he agreed to pay him to stay on as far as Livorno. By the time they arrived, he had offered him the chance to be a full member of the crew on *La Jeune Amelie's* next trip. Dantes knew that would take them close to the island of Monte Cristo, where Faria's treasure was buried. He agreed at once.

'Take some shore leave in Livorno,' said the captain, adding with a wry smile, 'It will give you the chance to get yourself cleaned up a bit!' He handed Dantes his wages. Dantes could not imagine any amount of treasure giving him as much joy as these first few coins which would secure his liberty.

He bought himself the traditional sailor's clothes sold in Italy, and went to the barbers. He joked that he had grown his hair and beard for a bet, and that he was looking forward to seeing his old face again. But when he looked in the mirror afterwards, he didn't recognize the man who gazed back at him.

His oval face was lengthened; his smiling mouth had firmed into a look of resolution. There were worry lines on his forehead, and his eyes were full of a deep sadness, which sometimes sparked with a flash of hatred. But everything he had been taught by Faria had given him an air of distinction too. His hair, washed and trimmed, was still black and glossy. With his toned body, he could even be said to have a certain aristocratic beauty. Dantes knew instantly that no one who remembered him as an innocent nineteen-year-old would think this could be the same person. That would make his plans for revenge much easier.

But it would take all his ingenuity to find his way to Monte Cristo.

Chapter 17
The Island of Monte Cristo

D antes signed up for three months on *La Jeune
Amelie*. In that time, travelling between Italy and
France with secret cargoes of luxurious fabrics and fine
foods, they would often pass the isle of Monte Cristo.
Dantes knew there was no point in going there until he
had the tools he would need to find the treasure, and
a way of getting it to the mainland. So he saved all the
money he earned, and happily fitted in with the rest of the
crew, teaching them everything he knew about the sea. He
was used to waiting, and he enjoyed being back in a world
so similar to the one he had adored before his arrest.

In the end, he got to Monte Cristo sooner than he
had planned. The smugglers needed to transfer a cargo of
contraband to another ship, and the captain chose Monte
Cristo for the handover. While *La Jeune Amelie* waited
for the other ship to arrive, the crew spread out across
the island. Dantes took a rifle, saying that he wanted to
go hunting and get something special for supper. He did
his best to go alone, but his friend Jacopo, the man who
had pulled him out of the water, insisted on coming, so
his search for the cave where the treasure was hidden was
furtive and interrupted many times. Even so, he noticed
some markings on the rocks that seemed to have been

made by a human hand. They appeared to be pointing towards a large boulder halfway up a steep slope. Dantes was desperate for a chance to investigate, but he needed to be alone.

A mountain goat, too unused to humans to be scared by them, pranced across his path. Dantes lifted his rifle and fired, and the animal died instantly.

Jacopo was thrilled. 'Well done, my friend. We will eat well tonight.'

'It's quite big,' said Dantes. 'We need to get it cooking soon.' Dantes saw a chance to get some solitude so that he could explore the rocks. 'Listen. I'd like to carry on hunting. Why don't you carry this back to the beach and get the fire started? You can signal to me when supper is ready, and I'll come back and join you.'

That sounded like a good idea to Jacopo, who happily left Dantes alone. Dantes made his way to the large boulder. Something in his bones told him it was blocking the mouth of the cave Faria had told him about. He tried levering the stone away with sticks, but it would not budge. He didn't realize how much time had passed until a blast on a horn from the sailors on the beach told him that supper was ready.

He started running across the jagged hilltop, back to the shoreline. The crew watched him as he leaped from rock to rock just as gracefully as the wild goats.

But suddenly, with a cry of agony, he fell away, out of sight. Jacopo was the first to run to find him. Dantes was gripping at his leg, writhing in pain. They carried him carefully to the beach, but with every step Dantes flinched and groaned, quietening down only when they had laid him on the shingle.

'We must get you back on board,' said the captain.

'No, sir. Please. Leave me here. Every movement hurts me. A ship is the last place I should be.'

'But we will have to sail tonight, as soon as we have offloaded the cargo. You know we have no time to lose after that.'

'Yes, I understand,' said Dantes. 'But I have an idea. Leave me here. Give me a supply of food, some tools to build a shelter, and some gunpowder in case I am attacked by animals. Give me a week to recover. Then, if you are passing, pick me up, or take some money from my pay to get a fishing boat to come for me. I am sure that in a week I will be able to bear the motion of the waves again.'

Jacopo pleaded to stay with him, but Dantes wouldn't hear of it. 'The ship will already be one man down without me. It wouldn't be fair to take you away when you are most needed.'

The captain was moved by Dantes's consideration for his shipmates, and vowed to return to pick him up. And so, after the other vessel had come and gone, *La Jeune*

Amelie sailed away. Once it was out of sight, Dantes leaped to his feet. The injury had been a sham. His trick had worked, and now he had plenty of time to find a way into the secret cave.

With the tools the crew had left him, he tried again to shift the boulder. It wouldn't budge. He had no experience with gunpowder and explosives, but the next morning, guessing where to place the charge, he gave it a try, packing powder around the stone, and then spilling out a trail across the ground so he could set off the blast from a distance. He went back to the beach, where the fire set to cook the goat was still smouldering. He set a branch alight and carried it up the mountain. As soon as Dantes put the flame to the powder, it raced along towards the huge rock, and blasted it away.

The boulder had indeed been hiding something, but it was not the yawning entrance to a cave. Instead, there was a flagstone set with a huge iron ring. Dantes struggled to lift it but at last it yielded, revealing, by the light of the burning torch, a stairway leading to an underground grotto. Surely this must be the cave where the Spadas had hidden their treasure back in the fifteenth century?

He climbed in. The air inside was thick and dank – worse even than in the dungeon of the Château d'If. The roof was low. There was no sign of any second chamber. Disappointment flooded through him. But he felt his way round the walls, tapping and listening for any sign that the rock had been disturbed. Back at the Château d'If, he and Faria had often feared that the guards might do the same, and find their secret. And suddenly, there it was: a different, hollower, sound. He felt with his fingers. A space had been filled in with stones. He brought his torch up close. The stones had been painted to look like granite. He worked away at them until there was room to get through. His heart was thundering with excitement, but he knew he had to wait to let some clean air get through before he could start digging in the far corner of the second chamber: the place where Faria's mysterious fragment of paper said the treasure would be.

After five or six blows, his spade hit something metallic. But whatever it was, it wasn't very wide. Alongside was something that gave a duller, softer sound, then further along the spade clinked again. Dantes worked out that he must be striking the top of a wooden chest bound with iron straps. Clearing the soil away and lifting the burning torch, he could make out a silver plate set into the centre of the lid. It was engraved with a picture of a sword against an oval shield. He knew at once what it was: the coat of arms of the Spada family. Faria had drawn it for him in prison, when telling the tale of the ancient Italian family. How could he ever have doubted Faria's sanity? If only his friend were there to share this moment!

A huge lock held the chest shut and it took a while for Dantes to break it away, but his excitement gave him the strength of many men. At last, the lid started to move. He closed his eyes as he lifted it fully open, remembering his beloved Faria and hoping, and fearing, that his life was about to change.

Chapter 18
The Treasure

The chest was divided into three sections. In the first, piles of ancient golden coins caught the light from Dantes's torch. The second was full of bars of unpolished gold; there was nothing attractive about them except their value. Dantes plunged his hand into the third compartment and pulled out diamonds, pearls and rubies, which, as he let them fall back into the box, made a sound like hail falling against glass. He tried to count the money, stopping when he was already in the millions. The jewellery was made of precious metals and rare stones, but it was clear that some pieces had been crafted by the greatest artists of their age. That would give them even more value. Stunned, Dantes wondered what to do.

It had grown dark outside while he had been attempting, unsuccessfully, to estimate his new wealth. He went back to the beach and ate a stale biscuit for his supper, then he lay down across the mouth of the cave to guard his fortune, even though he knew he was the only human on the island. When he woke the next morning, he had to go back inside to persuade himself that the events of the day before hadn't been a dream. For the rest of the week he constructed a new barricade to hide and protect the cave. While he was doing that, he thought out a plan of action. There was no way he could take the chest away with him. He would have to come back, alone, another time.

One morning, he saw the unmistakable shape of *La Jeune Amelie* on the horizon. He went into the grotto for one last time, and filled his pockets with precious stones. Then he sealed the entrance and climbed down to the beach to greet his friends. They were thrilled by his recovery, and he was glad to see them again. With Dantes steering the ship, they got back to Livorno faster than ever. Dantes was ready for revenge.

Chapter 19
The Legacy

In Livorno, Dantes sold four of his smallest stones for five thousand francs each. When he returned to the ship, he took the captain aside.

'I've had some news,' he said.

'Not too bad, I hope,' said the captain. 'You look very serious.'

'There has been a death in my family,' said Dantes, but he waved away the captain's sympathy. 'An uncle, a man I never met, has left me some money. I will never need to go to sea again.'

'So you want to leave *La Jeune Amelie*?'

'I do. But I will give you the money to find someone else.'

'Then of course you may go.'

'But I have another request. I want to take Jacopo with me. He saved my life and took care of me when I had nothing. I want to improve his life now.' He handed over a bulging purse. 'So here's enough for you to replace the two of us.'

'We always took you for some kind of nobleman, you know,' said the captain. 'Right from the start we knew there was something special about you. Not many sailors have your knowledge. I'm not surprised to hear that you had rich relatives.'

'Well, it has come as a surprise to me. My family hardly spoke of the man.'

'Nevertheless, you must make the most of your good fortune. And now you must surprise Jacopo, too. I sent him to clean the deck. He will be glad of the interruption.'

Anyone watching from the quayside would have been hard-pressed to work out what Dantes and Jacopo were talking about. They'd have seen a friendly greeting from Dantes, with Jacopo barely lifting his head from his mopping. Then Jacopo dropped the mop and stood gaping at his friend while Dantes talked at length, occasionally pointing out to sea. Finally, Jacopo fell to his knees, sobbing, as he clasped Dantes by the legs.

Had there been anyone near enough to hear, they would have known why the exchange was so emotional. Dantes was offering to buy Jacopo a ship and to give him enough money to hire a crew. There was only one condition: Jacopo's first journey must be to Marseille, where he should ask after an old man called Louis Dantes and a woman called Mercedes. He should then meet Dantes on Monte Cristo to tell him the result of his enquiries. They fixed a date for the reunion, and Dantes left *La Jeune Amelie* for the last time.

The next part of his plan involved buying a ship of his own, not a merchant ship this time, but a swift and stylish yacht he could sail by himself, or with the minimum of crewmen. He asked the boatbuilder for only one alteration in the design: the construction of a secret cupboard divided into three compartments, invisible to anyone who didn't know it was there.

Dantes sailed alone in this craft to meet Jacopo in Monte Cristo. The news from Marseille was that old Dantes was dead, and that Mercedes had long since left Marseille. No one knew where she was. Dantes was saddened, but not astounded by the news. Hoping that no one would recognize him, he set off for Marseille himself, ready to begin his campaign of revenge.

Chapter 20
Caderousse

After tying up his yacht at Marseille harbour, Dantes changed out of his sailor's clothes and put on a long flowing cloak. One of the first people he met on the quayside was a sailor who had served under him way back in 1815 on Monsieur Morrel's ship. The man treated him as a total stranger, and was happy to answer his questions about Danglars, Fernand and Caderousse. The only one of whom he had any knowledge was Caderousse, and he directed Dantes to the inn Caderousse now owned, some way out of town. Dantes pressed a coin into his hand to thank him. It was only later that that the man realized just how much it was worth.

As Dantes approached the inn, Caderousse was standing in the doorway, hoping that for once a customer would come by. He was pleased to see the traveller, and got him a bowl of soup.

'Sit with me, my good man,' said Dantes, 'for I have business you might be able to help me with.' Dantes was already sure who he was talking to, but he asked nevertheless.

'Am I right to think that your name is Gaspard Caderousse?'

'Indeed, sir,' said Caderousse, nervously. He feared that the man might have come about some unpaid debt. It was worse than that.

'My name is Busoni,' said Dantes, using the false name he had made up for the occasion. 'I have come here on behalf of someone I believe you once knew. Do you recognize the name Edmond Dantes?'

Caderousse was visibly shaken. 'Poor Edmond. Yes, I knew him. But I haven't seen him since 1815. Tell me, is he still alive?'

'He died a broken-hearted prisoner.'

Caderousse almost broke down. 'That is my fault,' he said. 'Edmond Dantes was an innocent man. I should have stopped his arrest. I could have spoken out afterwards. But I was weak. I was frightened. If he has sent you to get a confession from me, you have it now.'

Dantes was impressed by Caderousse's penitence, and touched, looking at his tatty clothes and the dilapidated inn, to see that fortune had been unkind to him over the years.

Caderousse spoke again. 'Did Edmond know that his father had died? The old man refused to eat after his son's arrest. Good Monsieur Morrel left money for him in a red silk purse on his mantelpiece. But the old man wouldn't touch it. He died of grief. I have that silk purse now. At least old Louis Dantes died without knowing who had betrayed his son.'

'Their names?'

'Danglars and Fernand.'

'The very men I was instructed to ask about!' said 'Busoni', with fake surprise. 'Tell me, what has become of them?'

Caderousse told him about their great success: Danglars as a banker in Paris, and Fernand in the military; and he broke the news that Fernand had married Mercedes.

'Your story is most troubling to me,' said 'Busoni', 'for Edmond asked me, with his dying breath, to come to Marseille to give money to five people: Old Dantes, yourself, Danglars, Fernand, and Mercedes. He believed you to be his greatest friends.'

'He had money, although he was a prisoner?' said Caderousse in disbelief.

'Not cash, but a diamond, passed to him in jail by another captive. I have instructions to sell the gem and to split the proceeds between you. I have the diamond with me now.'

'Busoni' took out the stone, and put it on the table. 'It is worth about fifty thousand francs, I am told. You were due a fifth of the proceeds, but with the death of old Dantes, and Mercedes's marriage, a third of that money should now be yours.'

'Dantes gave you this, and yet you have not kept it for yourself?' asked Caderousse.

No doubt that's what you would have done, thought 'Busoni'. But as he looked around him at the squalor in which his old neighbour now lived, his heart softened.

'I must fulfil the last wish of a dying man,' he said, remembering how much trouble that sentiment had caused him before. 'But if what you tell me is true, I do not think he would want me to follow his instructions to the letter.'

Caderousse's heart sank. Had he talked his way out of a share of a fortune? He was astounded by what 'Busoni' said next.

'Take the diamond. Keep it. The others do not deserve it now.' Caderousse grabbed for the stone. 'Busoni' closed his hand over Caderousse's. 'There is something I would like in return. You spoke of Monsieur Morrel.'

'Oh yes, he fought hard to find out what had happened to Edmond, and petitioned for his release. Poor Morrel. He is in trouble now. All his ships have gone down. He has impossible debts. His business is about to collapse, and just when his daughter is to be married. The young couple are going to start their life with nothing.'

'You said you have a red silk purse that Morrel gave old Louis Dantes?'

'I do.'

'May I take it? If you take the diamond?'

Caderousse couldn't get the purse quickly enough. It was empty.

'I'll be on my way,' said 'Busoni'.

Before the caped figure was halfway down the road, Caderousse's sour and greedy wife was at her husband's side. She had been eavesdropping on the conversation. Her eyes widened when she saw the diamond.

'I will go straight to Marseille to get it valued,' said Caderousse. 'That man told me it was worth fifty thousand francs.'

'Fifty thousand francs,' said his wife. An hour before, she had been penniless, but she was already dissatisfied. 'It is a large sum of money, but it is not a fortune!'

Chapter 21
The Prison Register

Dantes knew that money would damage Caderousse far more than any physical attack. So his generosity as 'Busoni' was not really a good deed at all. But he longed to do something genuinely kind with his wealth, and he wanted to do it quickly. First, he filled the red silk purse with money and left it, with a note saying it was from 'Sinbad the Sailor', for Monsieur Morrel's daughter. Then, dressed in the English fashion of the time – a bright blue frock coat, yellow trousers, and a white waistcoat – he went about paying off Monsieur Morrel's debts.

One of the people who had invested money in Morrel's business was the Inspector of Prisons. He was expecting to suffer badly if Morrel's company collapsed, so he was delighted when the Englishman, who introduced himself as 'Lord Wilmore', offered to pay handsomely to buy his share. Being in such a good mood, he saw no harm in granting a rather strange request. The Englishman asked to see the prison registers of the Château d'If.

'You see, I was educated in Rome by a learned man who suddenly disappeared. I subsequently learned that he had been imprisoned. His name was Faria. I would like to see the particulars of his case, since I am here.'

'Oh, Faria!' said the Inspector. 'There is a remarkable

story attached to him.' And he told the whole tale of Faria's death and Edmond's escape, and how the tunnel had been discovered afterwards.

'And the prisoner who was thrown over the battlements? Did he drown?' asked 'Lord Wilmore'.

'Undoubtedly. If his head was not cracked to pieces first,' laughed the Inspector, getting the prison register down from its shelf.

The Inspector left 'Lord Wilmore' leafing through the pages. He looked briefly at the notes on Faria, which told him nothing he didn't already know. Then, making sure he was not being watched, he turned to his own record.

There he found all the proof he needed. First, the original denunciation written by Danglars. He folded it up and put it in his pocket. In the book, he could see clearly that de Villefort had been behind his imprisonment, and had rejected a petition from Morrel calling for his release. Dantes saw himself described by de Villefort as: *An inveterate Bonapartist; took an active part in the return from the Isle of Elba. To be kept in complete solitary confinement, and to be strictly watched and guarded.*

At last, Dantes could be certain of the people against whom he should seek revenge. And meanwhile, Monsieur Morrel was astounded at the sudden happy transformation of his circumstances.

Chapter 22
Becoming the Count

Dantes often remembered Faria's warnings about becoming obsessed with revenge. The wise old man knew that the avenger could be damaged as much as his victim, and said that forgiveness and kind deeds were a surer route to happiness. Dantes had enjoyed helping Morrel, but he could not suppress his rage against his betrayers. He tried, and for nearly ten years he used his wealth purely as a source of enjoyment, making up for losing his youth to imprisonment by travelling and experiencing everything the world had to offer.

He mixed with everyone, high and low. Everywhere he went, people were impressed by his wealth and fascinated by his refusal to speak of his past. By 1838, when he was forty-two, he was known far and wide as the Count of Monte Cristo. If he had a home, it was his spectacularly lavish secret palace, built deep inside the rocks where he had found the treasure. His only companions there were the crew of his fantastic yacht, led by Jacopo: his dearest – indeed, his only – friend.

Through all those years, the men who had betrayed Dantes grew richer and more powerful. All except Caderousse. When he went to sell the diamond that 'Busoni' had given him, he thought of a way of doubling his money. The jeweller who had paid for it was found dead in his shop. Then Caderousse sold the diamond again, but he and his wife soon spent the proceeds. They argued. He killed her too, and he was put in prison. Dantes's 'gift' had done its job.

Though he travelled right across Europe, the Count of Monte Cristo kept away from Paris. He knew that de Villefort and Danglars were there, the first a leading judge, and the second a banker. Both were fabulously wealthy, but not as wealthy as the Count. He took his time working out how he would take revenge on them, but eventually he was unexpectedly presented with a good opportunity to enter their world.

It happened in Rome, where the Count had made friends with two young French aristocrats who were coming to the end of a long tour of Italy. Over coffee in a cafe near the Colosseum, one, called Franz, let slip a name the Count recognized at once.

'I'm dreading going home,' said Franz. 'My family are cooking up a wedding contract for me. I've got to marry de Villefort's daughter.'

'What's wrong with her?' asked his friend, Albert de Morcerf.

'Nothing much. She's nice enough looking. I hardly know her, to be honest. But who would want that dry old judge for a father-in-law, or her miserable old stepmother as a mother-in-law? I'm not ready to settle down to family life with anyone, let alone that particular family.'

'Well, we will just have to make the most of what time we have left in Rome,' said Albert. 'It's Carnival tonight; let's hire a carriage and get into the thick of things.'

'Gentlemen, I insist, take my carriage,' said the Count. 'But be careful. The streets of Rome can be dangerous at Carnival time. There are thieves on the loose, looking out for tourists like you.'

The young men promised to behave well, but by ten o'clock, Albert had got into a fight. Franz cowered in the coach as an ugly thug threatened his friend's life.

'Do you see that house over there?' shouted the brigand in thick Italian, pointing to a tumbledown shack next to an ancient church. 'Come there with a hundred gold coins by midnight, or your friend will die.'

Franz raced back to the mansion that the Count of Monte Cristo had rented in Rome. Sweating and shaking with terror, Franz explained that although he was from a rich family, he had spent most of the money they had given him for his travels.

'And in any case,' he said, 'where would I find gold coins at this time of night?'

'Have no fear,' said Monte Cristo. 'I always keep cash close at hand. I will take the money to Albert's captors.' He asked Franz to describe the gang's hideout. 'I know the area,' said the Count. 'You wait here. You have had a shock.'

In the alley alongside the house where Albert was held, no one saw the Count huddled with the bandits' leader. Nobody heard Monte Cristo's promise to protect the gang from the police if they swore to help him in the future. As far as Albert knew, Monte Cristo was simply a hero who had generously bought his freedom. For the Count, the episode had been an opportunity to bind two very different people into his quest for revenge: Albert, the French aristocrat who could lead him to his prey; and the brigand leader, who might one day be called upon to inflict a punishment.

Soon after midnight, Albert and Franz were safely reunited at Monte Cristo's house. 'I blame myself,' said the Count. 'My grand carriage was bound to attract attention. Please accept my apologies for putting you at risk.'

'No, no,' said Albert. 'I insulted the man. I picked the fight. What can I do to thank you for saving my life?'

The Count was impressed by young Albert's honesty. He didn't have much time for Franz, whom he found shallow and weak, but he was taken with the other young man, and felt he would like to spend more time in his company.

'There is one thing you could do for me,' he said.

'Anything,' said Albert. 'Just ask.'

'I have been meaning for some time to visit Paris,' said the Count, reflecting in his own mind that it was almost a quarter of a century since his errand with the letter from Elba would have taken him there. 'If you are going home soon, might I come with you? I know nobody there. Would you introduce me into Parisian society?'

'It would be an honour,' said Albert. And before the end of the week they were on their way.

Chapter 23
Paris

Albert made arrangements for some of his closest friends to meet the Count at his apartment near his parents' mansion in Paris. Albert's tales of the extraordinary Count had intrigued them, though they doubted whether such a fascinating man could be real, or if he was, whether he would turn up. But Monte Cristo arrived and charmed all the guests, including Maximilian Morrel, the son of the Marseille shipowner, who was now in the army. Maximilian did not recognize Monte Cristo as Dantes, but Monte Cristo studied him closely, finding him, like his father, to be an excellent man.

When the guests had gone, Albert showed Monte Cristo round his apartment. The main room was decorated with modern pictures, and Albert was impressed at the way Monte Cristo could identify the artists responsible for even the most recently painted. He seemed to know as much about the modern world as he did about the ancient.

Then, unseen by Albert, Monte Cristo froze. One of the paintings had given him a physical shock. It was a portrait of a young woman wearing the picturesque costume of a Catalan fisherwoman, with a red and gold bodice, and golden pins in her lustrous black hair. She was gazing out at the sea. It looked just like Mercedes, as Edmond remembered her, long ago, back in Marseille. He recovered his composure and complimented Albert on the picture and its subject.

'This is a most charming young woman, Albert. Do you know her? Is her costume for a fancy-dress ball?'

'It is a costume, but it's not a girlfriend of mine. It's my mother. She had this portrait painted some years ago as a surprise for my father, who was away at the war. As you can see, it is one of the artist's greatest works. For that reason, my father would not get rid of it, but he hates it, and that is why I have it here. Whenever my mother comes to visit, it makes her cry. I don't know why.'

Talk of his parents prompted Albert to ask the Count whether he would like to meet them. Monte Cristo could hardly say no, and he and Albert were soon walking across the courtyard to the mansion of the Count and Countess of Morcerf. As a servant went to announce their arrival, Monte Cristo and Albert waited by a lavish portrait of a dashing soldier decorated with many medals. A moment later, a door opened and the subject of the painting walked in. In an instant, the inkling of recognition Monte Cristo had felt on seeing the picture was confirmed.

The passage of time, years of warfare and the acquisition of great wealth could not fully disguise Fernand, the fisherman who had been Monte Cristo's rival in love years ago in Marseille. Morcerf, on the other hand, saw nothing familiar about the elegant middle-aged man who stood before him.

Albert introduced them, unaware that Monte Cristo's mind was wrestling with the realization that the Count of Morcerf had once been Fernand, and that, quite by chance, he had stumbled upon one of his betrayers. Even more unsettling was the thought that Albert was his son.

Morcerf bowed. 'My good sir, I must thank you for saving Albert's life. My wife will be down shortly, and I know she wants to express her gratitude for your heroism, too.'

Monte Cristo nodded silently, all the while thinking of the portrait in Albert's apartment. Albert's mother must be Mercedes, and proud Morcerf's reason for hating the picture of her must be that it reminded him of their humble origins. There was a rustle of skirts and she entered, only to fall into a swoon when she saw Monte Cristo.

'Forgive me, sir,' she said, regaining her composure and clinging on to social niceties to stop herself from giving way completely. 'I was overcome to meet the man who saved me from the depths of despair by rescuing my son.'

Monte Cristo was in no doubt that she had recognized him as Dantes, just as he was sure that she was Mercedes. Time, education and wealth had transformed her in many ways, but the essence of the girl he had loved was still there.

The three of them talked formally about Monte Cristo's visit to Paris and how they must all get together, often. Monte Cristo could see sadness in Mercedes's eyes. She could see pain and anger in his. Then Mercedes said she needed to lie down, and the Count of Morcerf had to leave for an appointment, so their meeting was mercifully cut short.

Monte Cristo took his leave of Albert. On the way home he pondered what revenge he might take against Morcerf. Was there anything he could do without hurting Mercedes and Albert, too? Morcerf had spoken with great pride about how he had now left the army and entered parliament. Surely no one could move from being a fisherman to becoming a Count and having a role in the government without doing something nefarious along the way? Monte Cristo was already planning to send out spies and to keep his ear to the ground as he mixed with the people who had caused him to suffer so much. He would pay special attention to any rumours about Morcerf.

And, with regret, he resolved to respect the clear signal that Mercedes had silently transmitted in their brief encounter. He was sure that, as a respectable married woman, she wanted nothing to do with him now. After nearly a quarter of a century of longing, it was almost more than he could bear.

Chapter 24
Overheard Plans

Monte Cristo was soon a sensation in Paris. Everyone was swept away by his wealth, his charm and the atmosphere of mystery that surrounded his origins. He hated the round of balls and parties in which every hostess fought to involve him, but he had to take part. For it turned out that the people he most wanted to see, Danglars and de Villefort, were part of the same social set. To find a way of undermining each of them, it was necessary only to get to know their friends. Gossip was rife, and everyone wanted to get closer to Monte Cristo by offering him titbits of dirt about their closest acquaintances. He soon put away thoughts of murdering his betrayers. It would be far more interesting to watch them destroy themselves.

He started with the de Villeforts. Monsieur de Villefort was now the leading prosecutor in France, respected as an unbending upholder of the law. Was there anything he cared for more than his life? The answer was clear: his position and reputation. That was where Monte Cristo would aim his attack.

The woman de Villefort had married on the day he sent Dantes to prison had died, leaving behind a daughter, Valentine. His second wife was bitter and ambitious. She

ill-treated the girl, and favoured her own son. At tea
parties and dances, Monte Cristo studied them all. He
could see that Valentine was unhappy but he did not
understand why until, on a whim one day, he tried to track
down Maximilian Morrel. As he arrived, he recognized
Maximilian's voice from over the high garden wall. 'But
you can't marry him!' The young man sounded just like
his father, the kind shipowner who had fought so hard to
save Dantes from prison years ago.

'I've got no choice,' said a woman. 'Even though I don't
love him, my father can't resist the idea of me sharing
Franz's money.'

'I can't offer you riches,' said Maximilian. 'But we could
live comfortably together on my salary. Why don't we
run away?'

'We can't. My grandfather is ill. He's had a stroke. He
can't speak and he can hardly move. I couldn't bear to
leave him.'

'Could we meet at his house?' Maximilian asked.

There was a pause. 'If we were careful.'

'When will you be there?'

'Tomorrow afternoon,' said the girl.

'Tell me the address.'

'Rue Coq-Héron, 13.'

At once, Monte Cristo knew that the girl must be
Valentine de Villefort and that the grandfather to whom

she was so loyal was the republican, Noirtier. All Monte Cristo's troubles stemmed from agreeing to deliver a letter to him. After nearly twenty-five years, the address on that letter started pulsing through his memory again: *Rue Coq-Héron, 13.* Perhaps he should go there. Maybe the old invalid would be the key to engineering de Villefort's downfall.

This was clearly no time to make an unannounced call on Maximilian. Monte Cristo's heart ached at the thought that he would have to put a stop to his liaison with Valentine. How could the son of the man who had believed in Edmond Dantes's innocence love the daughter of the person who had condemned him to the Château d'If?

Later that day, in a corner at a social gathering, Monte Cristo found himself in conversation with Valentine's stepmother, Madame de Villefort.

'I've been checking up on you,' she said, with a little giggle. 'I have been corresponding with a friend in Italy.'

'And what have you found out?' Monte Cristo asked, trying not to sound alarmed.

'I am told that you are an expert on medicines.'

'Hardly. I once knew a man who told me some ancient secrets, that's all,' said Monte Cristo, remembering Faria.

'Really, Count, you underestimate yourself. I hear stories from Italy that you make a potion which can restore life to the dying.'

Monte Cristo had indeed once used the most powerful of Faria's concoctions to save someone's life. 'That mixture can work wonders,' he said. 'But it must be handled with care. In large doses it can also kill.'

'And this recipe is secret?'

Monte Cristo stayed quiet. Giving poison to Madame de Villefort was not to be done lightly. On the other hand, were she to be convicted of murder, her husband's career would be shattered. And if she were to use it on de Villefort himself ...

He finally answered her. 'I might be prepared to divulge it.'

'At what price?'

'Not for money. In exchange for some information.'

'About what?

'About the Count of Morcerf, and Baron Danglars.'

Madame de Villefort fluttered her fan. 'Oh yes,' she said. 'I think I could manage that.'

'Then I will bring the formula when you next invite me to dine,' said Monte Cristo with a smile. 'But of course, it is only to be used as a medicine, not as a poison.'

Madame de Villefort replied with a coquettish giggle. 'My dear Count, what are you suggesting?'

Anyone looking on would have imagined that their little talk had featured nothing but gentle social chit-chat.

Chapter 25
Baron Danglars

Most of Madame de Villefort's gossip about Baron Danglars was unsurprising: he was motivated entirely by money and was always willing to lend, as long as his creditors paid him far more in return. Monte Cristo saw at once that one way to hit him would be to pose as a reputable borrower, and then to fail to pay the debt. In his various disguises, using false names and with forged recommendations from respectable banks, he drew a small fortune from Danglars's coffers.

But he could also see that there were other ways to get at the greedy banker. For a start, there was his wife.

'They don't love each other,' said Madame de Villefort. 'They live separate lives. And she helps herself to his money, too. So far, she has been lucky. She has a contact in the government who feeds her sensitive information. By secretly moving Danglars's money around on the stock market she has made herself quite a fortune.'

Monte Cristo did not like Madame Danglars. She was proud and scheming. He fancied the idea of using her to bring her husband down. He arranged for a false report to arrive on the desk of her contact in the government. It said that revolution was about to break out in Spain.

Madame Danglars rushed to tell her husband to sell all

his Spanish bonds. For one night, he gloated at the fools who had bought the worthless scraps of paper. But the next day, the rumour of revolution was proved false, and values changed. Danglars lost more than a million francs, and his reputation as a safe pair of banking hands was demolished. But he was not yet completely ruined. Monte Cristo was still working on that.

Chapter 26
The Count of Morcerf

Madame de Villefort's information about Fernand, Count of Morcerf, was less helpful to Monte Cristo. She talked of him mainly as an upstart soldier who had wormed his way into high society using his wealth. She hinted that his money must have been acquired dishonestly, but Monte Cristo already assumed that. It was one of Monte Cristo's spies who came up with facts that might threaten Morcerf's position as a decorated military man and rising political star.

The spy arrived at Monte Cristo's mansion with a young woman. She was beautiful, and spoke with a foreign accent.

'Where are you from?' asked Monte Cristo.

'I come from a far corner of the French Empire,' she said. 'My father was in charge there. Some years ago, when I was still a child, French troops were sent to help him defend our lands.'

Monte Cristo could guess what was coming next. 'And one of the soldiers was called Morcerf?'

The girl looked bewildered. 'No, sir. I have come to tell you about a man named Fernand.'

'Of course,' said Monte Cristo. 'That was his name before he had his title, and his wealth.'

'He had no money at all when I knew him,' said the girl.

'My father provided for him, fought alongside him and taught him new military skills.'

'So where is your father now?'

The girl's eyes dropped. 'Dead, sir. And dead because of Fernand's treachery. Fernand did a deal with the enemy: accepting money in exchange for my father's life. He took my father's fortune too, and sold me and my mother into servitude.'

'Have you any proof of this?' asked the Count.

'No, but I can give you the names of people who can confirm my story.'

Monte Cristo turned to the spy who had brought the girl to his house. 'Who else knows about this?' he said.

'No one, sir. I have not allowed her to speak with anybody since we reached Paris, and you know that my lips are sealed.'

'I will give you both shelter here for the time being,' said Monte Cristo. 'This matter must go to law.' He turned to the girl. 'Mademoiselle, are you prepared to testify against Fernand in court?'

'Yes, sir.'

'Tomorrow, I will arrange for a journalist friend of mine to come to talk to you. I want you both to tell him everything you know about this matter, and to put him on to anyone else who can back up this story. Do you understand?'

The spy nodded.

'Yes, sir. Thank you,' said the girl.

'I promise you, your wait for justice will not be long,' said the Count. He rang for a servant to conduct them to guest rooms at the back of the house. The footman arrived with a silver tray bearing a calling card. It was Maximilian Morrel's.

'Shall I send him away, sir?' asked the footman, for he could see that the Count was involved in something very serious.

'No,' said the Count. 'Tell him to wait in the library. I will go to see him directly.'

Chapter 27
Noirtier and Danglars

Maximilian had no idea that the Count of Monte Cristo had saved his father's shipping business, nor that he had left the mysterious red velvet purse of money for his sister. But he had taken an instant liking to the Count when he had met him at Albert's apartment. Now he was asking for help.

'I believe, sir, that when you were in Rome, you met Albert's friend, Franz?'

'I did. But why is that of concern to you?'

'You may not know that Franz is to be betrothed to Valentine, the daughter of Monsieur de Villefort.'

'I had heard,' said the Count.

Maximilian was prepared to tell the whole story of how he and Valentine were in love, and to ask for the Count's help to make their marriage possible, but Monte Cristo interrupted him. He saw an opportunity to get behind the scenes in de Villefort's household and perhaps to bring the grand judge down sooner than he had hoped.

'Maximilian, I am sure that Franz does not want to marry Valentine. His desire to avoid a wedding is just as strong as your wish to have one. If you were intending to ask me to plead your case with Valentine's parents, I am more than willing to do so, but I suggest we steer clear of them for now. Do you by any chance know Monsieur Noirtier, Valentine's grandfather?'

Maximilian was thrown. To admit to associating with a republican revolutionary could be dangerous.

Monte Cristo continued. 'Have no fear. I am not trying to trap you. I have my own reasons for wanting to see him, and I wonder whether you might arrange an introduction.'

'He is old and frail. A stroke has robbed him of movement and speech. Only Valentine and his faithful attendant, Barrois, can understand him. Valentine is alone with him now.'

'Then perhaps she can act as my interpreter,' said Monte Cristo. 'I will speak to him about your future, and this seems an ideal time to do it.'

They walked together to Rue Coq-Héron. The Count imagined how he might have made the same journey with the letter all those years ago. When they got to the old man's chamber, Monte Cristo introduced himself.

'I am the Count of Monte Cristo. I have matters of great sensitivity that I wish to tell you about. With your agreement, Monsieur Noirtier, I would like to be alone with you for a while. Would it be possible for you to allow that, and for Valentine and Maximilian to return in half an hour?'

Only Valentine could understand Noirtier's response.

'He says yes. We will wait in the room downstairs. Call us if you need us. Remember, he has perfect hearing and understanding, even though he cannot reply to you.'

The door closed behind them, and the Count began.

'You will have guessed, sir, that I have come to plead for the happiness of those two young people, and that is indeed part of my purpose, but only part. On that subject, I suggest that you change your will. Your attendant can dictate it to a lawyer. Write that you will give all your money to the poor unless Valentine marries Maximilian, in which case everything will go to her. Make sure that your son, de Villefort, and his wife know of this. It may be enough to make them call off the marriage contract with Franz.'

Monte Cristo looked for a response from the old man. Noirtier was totally still, but there seemed to be a light in his eyes. 'I cannot tell what you are thinking, sir. You may be grateful to your son, de Villefort, for keeping you hidden from your enemies, despite your political sympathies. I want to tell you of something else he did, which was undoubtedly to his own advantage, but may have been for your benefit too. I suffered because of de Villefort's action, and I think you should know of it. I have to take you back many years, to February 1815.'

Monte Cristo told the old man all about the letter from Elba and the Château d'If. 'I tell you this because

I want you to know, in case you don't already, the monstrous things of which your son is capable. Should his fortunes change in the near future, you may guess who has orchestrated his fall. But I bear you no ill-will, and so I warn you, should you receive a visit from Madame de Villefort before your new will is sealed, do not drink any liquids she may serve you, and get your assistant to wash out every glass after she has gone.'

He paused, and looked again for a reaction on the old man's frozen face. In case Noirtier had not fully understood, he carried on.

'You probably already know how Madame de Villefort favours her own son over her stepdaughter, Valentine. I have reason to believe that she has access to poison, and that she would stop at nothing to prevent you leaving everything to Valentine, or giving your fortune to the poor. You cannot be too careful. Believe me. I wish you no harm.'

Monte Cristo called Valentine and Maximilian back upstairs. 'I will leave you together now,' he said. 'I have another call to make.'

The Count went straight to Danglars's mansion. The banker was sitting at his desk, surrounded by ledgers and scraps of paper.

'Ah, Monte Cristo. So you are not ashamed to visit me. All my other friends seem to have fallen away.'

'And how is Madame Danglars bearing up to your misfortune?' asked the Count, trying to sound sincere.

'She has gone. I don't know where. It appears she has been squirrelling away money of her own. She is not willing to give it to me in my time of trouble.'

'I have come to donate money to the children's hospital,' said Monte Cristo. 'I understand that you hold their account. I have signed orders for five million francs. But you will have to cash them at my bank in Rome.'

Danglars's eyes brightened. A trip to Rome was a small inconvenience for such a prize. Monte Cristo was in no doubt that the hospital had little chance of receiving the money. As soon as he got home, he sent someone else to Rome: a servant with instructions for some people who owed him a favour. They were the very bandits who had captured Albert on the night of the Carnival.

Chapter 28
The Newspaper

After the tip-off from Monte Cristo's spy, it didn't take long for the newspaper to flesh out the story about the Count of Morcerf's treachery and corruption in the army.

Albert wanted to take the paper to court for blackening his father's name, but Monte Cristo persuaded him to wait to see whether the public prosecutor thought there was enough evidence to bring charges. At lunch at the de Villeforts' house, the Count found out that the answer was yes.

'I cannot give you confidential information, of course,' said de Villefort, 'but I would not be surprised if the Count of Morcerf eventually found his way behind bars.'

'And you don't feel awkward, mounting a case against one of your friends?' asked Monte Cristo.

'It makes no difference,' said de Villefort. 'My role is to make sure that the law takes its proper course, whatever the circumstances. I have interviewed the poor girl whose father was betrayed and cheated by Morcerf when he was wearing the uniform of France. I cannot let the crime go unpunished.'

'But if he could prove his innocence?'

'He will have his chance to do that in court. I would

never send an innocent man to prison. Justice must be done.'

Monte Cristo stopped himself saying anything. He was not yet ready to confront de Villefort about the miscarriage of justice he had perpetrated so many years ago.

By now, Noirtier's will had been rewritten to say that everything would go to the poor unless Valentine married Maximilian, but de Villefort was still refusing to call off her betrothal to the wealthy Franz. So Monte Cristo was not surprised to see that Valentine was only picking at her food over lunch.

'Are you ill?' asked her father. 'You are looking pale, my dear.'

'I do feel a little strange,' said Valentine. 'All drinks taste bitter to me.'

'You should go to bed,' said her stepmother. Then she changed the subject, asking her husband, 'What do you think Morcerf's wife and son will do if he is disgraced? Surely his possessions will be confiscated. All his money was made in the service of the state. The government will take it back.'

Monte Cristo had been hit by two blows. He guessed that Madame de Villefort was trying to poison Valentine by giving her the secret potion little by little; and he knew that Albert and Mercedes were going to suffer because he had taken revenge on Fernand. He didn't know what to do first. Should he warn Valentine, or rush to the Morcerf house to explain everything?

He tried to get Valentine away from her stepmother. 'Do you need some air, Valentine?' he asked. 'I could take you for a walk if you like.'

Madame de Villefort put down her knife and fork. 'Thank you, Count, but I will take Valentine upstairs. A rest will do her good.'

Without creating a scene, there was nothing Monte Cristo could do to stop Madame de Villefort leaving the room with Valentine. But now, at last, he was alone with de Villefort. Was this the moment to reveal his true identity? *Not yet*, he decided. It was more important to get to the Morcerfs' mansion before Fernand was arrested. He could return later with the antidote to the poison and revive Valentine if it had already taken full effect.

'Forgive me, Monsieur de Villefort,' he said politely. 'I feel I am intruding on your womenfolk. Thank you for a delightful lunch. I will take my leave.'

De Villefort, oblivious to Monte Cristo's torment, was happy to end the meal early. He had signed the arrest warrant for Morcerf before they had sat down to eat, and he wanted to interview the captive as soon as possible.

Chapter 29
Too Late

Monte Cristo raced to the Morcerf mansion, but he was too late. Albert answered the front door.

'The guards came for my father,' he said. 'They say that those newspaper stories are true.'

'I know they are,' said the Count. 'Albert, you must be strong for your mother now that your father is in prison.'

'But he isn't!' said Albert. 'He wasn't man enough for that. He has gone. All he left was this note.'

He showed Monte Cristo a thick sheet of paper, bearing the elaborate Morcerf crest. It was the last token of the family's grandeur. The words had been scribbled in haste.

I have gone
Do not follow me.
No one will ever see me again.

'What a coward!' said Albert. 'He has left us to bear his disgrace alone.'

'May I see your mother?' said the Count.

'You will find her in the garden,' replied Albert.

Mercedes turned as Monte Cristo stepped through the French windows. She had been crying.

'Oh, Edmond!' she said.

Edmond. It was the first time he had been called by

that name since Faria had died in the prison. Mercedes alone, of all the people who had known him in his youth, had recognized him behind the mysterious exterior of the Count of Monte Cristo. But he knew from a sternness in her manner that they would never be together.

'You knew it was me?' he asked.

'From the first moment I saw you. But Edmond, you are so changed. You are cold and hard. So distant. Not at all the young man I once loved.'

'Will you gather your possessions together and go away?' he asked.

'No. I am no Madame Danglars. Nothing here is rightfully mine. But Albert and I will leave Paris.'

'Where will you go?

'Back to Marseille. I have been poor there before, and I will be poor there again. Now leave, Edmond. Go, please.'

Monte Cristo did as he was told. On the way out, he told Albert to visit the Post Office in Marseille when they arrived. A letter would be waiting for him.

'I don't understand.'

'You will, Albert. Now take care of your mother. She needs you.'

Monte Cristo didn't want to leave the Morcerf house, but he knew he should find out whether Valentine de Villefort was safe. Stopping only to collect an antidote to the poison from his home, he made his way back to the de Villeforts' residence. He told the footman that he had urgent news for the Chief Prosecutor.

'What is it?' said de Villefort, emerging into the hall.

'The Count of Morcerf has gone.'

'Is that all?' said de Villefort. 'My men told me a few minutes ago.'

'But there is something else.'

'Another time. I am busy.'

'Check on Valentine now,' urged Monte Cristo.

'My wife is with her.'

'That is why you must go up to her. Believe me; your daughter's life is in danger.'

De Villefort walked towards the grand staircase. Monte Cristo's instinct was to push past him and rush to Valentine's aid, but cold revenge urged him to let de Villefort discover the scene upstairs for himself. He followed as the judge climbed to Valentine's room, and couldn't help enjoying de Villefort's howl of pain as he found his daughter lying dead across her bed.

'She has been poisoned,' said Monte Cristo.

'Who did this?' said de Villefort. Collapsed in the bedside chair, with his head in his hands, he couldn't see Monte Cristo pouring drops of the antidote into Valentine's mouth.

Monte Cristo knew that the antidote would take half an hour to work, if it worked at all. He had plenty of time to reduce the grand man to nothing, in his own eyes, and in the eyes of the world.

De Villefort was rocking backwards and forwards, tortured by grief. 'Who did this?' he cried again.

'Whoever it was, they must face justice,' said Monte Cristo.

'Yes, yes, of course. The full might of the law must be used.'

'Whoever it was?'

'Regardless of wealth, status, or family,' said de Villefort. 'No one is above the law.'

'Then you must prosecute your wife for the worst of all possible crimes. For she is the culprit. I locked the door to her room on my way up here. She is captured. Justice can take its course. But when it does, your own reputation will be ruined.'

De Villefort was weeping. 'You are a cruel, evil man,' he said.

'No, Monsieur de Villefort. You are the one who is cruel and evil. Do you remember the day you married your first wife?'

'Of course,' said de Villefort, mystified.

'Do you recall a young seaman arrested and imprisoned on your orders, without trial?'

'I can't remember every case, after all these years,' muttered de Villefort.

'Then maybe this will refresh your memory,' said the Count, thrusting into de Villefort's hands the anonymous note he had stolen from the prison records in Marseille.

'Where did you get this?'

'From inside a register which proves beyond doubt that the innocent Edmond Dantes was imprisoned in the Château d'If for fourteen years to save your career, and to prevent your father from facing justice. Dantes would still be in a dank dungeon, if he had not escaped.'

De Villefort was shaking. 'Where is he now?' he said, raising his head to look into the Count's eyes.

The Count stared back and, as he did so, de Villefort saw before him not Monte Cristo, but the nineteen-year-old Edmond Dantes, the man whose life he had wrecked.

The Count of Monte Cristo knew at that moment that de Villefort's mind had gone. Faced with the prospect of losing his family, his reputation, his power and prestige, the prosecutor was destroyed by madness as surely as if he had been put to death.

Chapter 30
Paying the Price

Monte Cristo carried Valentine's body through a back door and into his own house. She was starting to show signs of life again. He sent for Maximilian, but told him nothing of what had happened. Instead, he asked if he would do an errand for him.

'Of course,' said Maximilian. 'Anything.'

'I want you to take this letter.' It was addressed to Albert de Morcerf in Marseille.

'I'll go right away,' said Maximilian. 'The Post Office is on my way to Noirtier's, anyway. I'm meeting Valentine there tonight.'

'No. I want you to take the letter all the way to Marseille. And then you are to hire a boat and to meet me on the isle of Monte Cristo in one month's time. Do not speak to anyone in Paris. Go straight away. My carriage is ready for you.'

'But—'

'Please. No questions, Maximilian. Trust me. You said you would do anything.'

'And I will.'

The letter to Albert told him to dig by the tree in the garden of the little house where Edmond Dantes's father had once lived. There he would find a box containing the small sum that Dantes had put aside to start married life with Mercedes.

Almost everything was done. But Monte Cristo had not finished with Danglars. The banker had gone to Italy to collect Monte Cristo's five million francs, but the thieves who had once attacked Albert were waiting for him. Monte Cristo had paid them to hold Danglars captive and teach him a lesson.

He was kept in conditions that were luxurious compared with the horrors of the Château d'If, but it was still a shock for the stout and greasy banker to find himself on a cold hard floor, with only vermin for company. He was experiencing just a tiny taste of what Edmond Dantes had endured because of him. But Edmond was not the only Dantes who had suffered at Danglars's hands. Because of him, old Louis Dantes had starved to death, and now it was Danglars's turn to find out what that was like.

His captors refused him food for several days, finally relenting by presenting him with a hot and delicious roast chicken. Just as Danglars was about to plunge in his fork, the jailer pulled it away.

'Hold!' he cried. 'You have not paid!'

'Paid?' said Danglars. 'No one said anything about paying.'

The guard shrugged, and started to walk away, but

Danglars called him back and threw a small coin in his direction.

'That's not enough,' said the guard. 'You owe me another four thousand nine hundred and ninety-nine.'

Danglars laughed. But in the end he paid up, and each day his dinner cost him more, until the five million francs he had stolen from the hospital fund were almost all used up. He couldn't bear to part with his last fifty thousand.

'I would rather die than lose all my money,' he cried.

A man in a cloak with a large hood appeared. In a slow, booming voice he called out to Danglars.

'Do you repent?'

'Of what must I repent?' asked Danglars.

'Of the evil you have done,' said the hooded man.

'Oh, yes! Oh, yes, I repent!' said Danglars.

'Then I forgive you,' said the man, throwing off his hood and stepping into the light.

'The Count of Monte Cristo!' cried Danglars.

'You are mistaken. I am not the Count of Monte Cristo. I am the man you betrayed so that you could raise yourself a fortune. I am the man whom you condemned to die of hunger in a prison far worse than this. I am Edmond Dantes!'

Danglars screamed and fell to the ground.

'I am done with you,' said Dantes. 'You can keep the little money you have left. I have restored the five million to the hospital. These men will give you a good meal, for which I will pay.'

When Danglars had eaten his fill, the brigands followed Monte Cristo's instructions and dumped him at a roadside, leaning against a tree. Danglars stayed there all night, not knowing where he was. When dawn broke, he saw he was near a stream, and dragged himself towards it to drink. As he stooped towards the water, he saw his reflection. His hair had turned quite white.

Chapter 31
New Horizons

Maximilian kept his word and delivered the letter to Marseille. Then he made his way to the isle of Monte Cristo. The Count's faithful servant, Jacopo, saw his boat approaching and led him to the wonderful palace deep within the rocks.

Monte Cristo greeted him warmly, but told him at once that he had serious news. He described how Madame de Villefort had poisoned Valentine. The shock to Maximilian was so great that he could hardly hear the rest of the details: how the Count himself had saved her from death, and how she was here, now, waiting for Maximilian.

They had a grand dinner, during which the Count revealed his whole story: from his arrest in 1815 to the destruction of the men who had betrayed him.

'I have learned so much,' he said. 'I know now that revenge does not bring satisfaction, and that the greatest happiness can only be experienced by those who have known the greatest despair. And I believe that all human wisdom can be contained in these words: "wait and hope."'

In the morning, Valentine and Maximilian went for a walk along the sea shore. Jacopo came towards them with a letter. 'From the Count,' he said.

Maximilian opened it, and read it to Valentine.

My dear Maximilian,

A boat is waiting for you, and Jacopo will sail you to Livorno, where Monsieur Noirtier is waiting to see his granddaughter. He wants to wish you both well for your wedding.

Everything on this island, and my house in Paris, are my wedding gifts to you. I ask only that Valentine should give everything she inherits from her family to the poor.

Your friend,
Edmond Dantes
Count of Monte Cristo

Valentine turned to Jacopo. 'Where is the Count?' she asked. 'We must thank him.'

'Look,' said Jacopo, pointing out to sea.

On the blue line separating the sky from the sea they could see a large white sail.

'Will we ever see him again?' said Maximilian.

'We must do what he has just told us to do,' said Valentine. 'Wait and hope!'